THE
WATERMEN
OF THE CHESAPEAKE BAY

ISBN 0-9603486-0-3

THE
WATERMEN
OF THE CHESAPEAKE BAY

BY JOHN HURT WHITEHEAD, III

For Aunt Laura, who first showed me the Bay . . .
and how to bait a crab line. And who always had
faith that I would do something worthwhile.

I want to thank all of you who took the time to talk with me or endure the discomfort of being photographed. Space doesn't allow me to name each of you individually, and you probably prefer it that way, but I'll always remember your kindness and generosity.

You may see your friends or your neighbors or yourself in these pages, and nearby, the words of someone 100 miles away. The words and the pictures have been grouped here by subject matter, so please don't assume that someone said the words nearest his picture.

If you should be traveling my way, please stop in and let me know how things are going with you. I'll do the same. One way or another, I hope we'll all see each other again.

INTRODUCTION

I must have presented a strange and humorous sight to him as I carefully approached on the rickety pier, arms slightly extended for balance. Cameras and tape recorders and bags hung from straps around my neck and shoulders, and my right hand tightly gripped a shiney new lunch box. I leaned over his boat and made the request that I would repeat hundreds of times over the next three years. "Hi, I'm doing a book about the Watermen of the Bay, and would greatly appreciate it if you'd allow me to go along with you and take some photographs". The older waterman looked at me and then at the floor boards of his boat. His leathery face eased into a smile. "Son", he said, looking up, "You as welcome to go with me as a cool breeze in August, but I ought to tell you, I don't go nowhere near them old houses you fellows are always writing about". I started to explain and he continued. "and all of them sailing skipjack boats are up the Bay a ways. You ain't going to get no pictures of one of them around here. All you'd see today is a worn out old man trying to make a living off the water". It seemed somehow too difficult to explain that the beauty I was seeking wasn't in their ancestor's homes or their antique boats but in their own faces and hands and humor. I simply said, "Well, maybe I'll learn something too". . . . "Now, that you might, sonny boy, that you might" he said with an affirmative nod and a wink. "If you ain't afraid that this face is going to break one of them Kodaks, you come on aboard. You don't look like you'd do me a bit of harm in the world".

Similar situations have occured many times since then and in all parts of the Bay. The watermen didn't always understand why someone wanted to do a book about them, but being the gentleman that they are, they welcomed me aboard anyway. I was never given excuses about insurance regulations or Coast Guard rules. The strongest turndown I ever received was, "Cap'n, can you come back one day after I get her off the railway and cleaned up".

They've stumbled over me and my equipment smiling and endured the discomfort of being photographed a hundred times a day, while trying to work. They've tried to explain, in terms I could understand, everything about which I inquired. I always took my lunch along, but rarely ate it, as they were so insistant that I share their food, especially when they cooked on board. When a plate of crisp fried oysters, fresh from the bottom, is thrust at you along side a bowl of blackeyed peas and tomatoes and homemade biscuits, you tend to forget about your vienna sausage and potato sticks and your determination not to impose.

I've been invited into their homes and their churches and met their families over dinner. I've taken home oysters by the bushel, clams by the hundred, soft and hard crab, fish of all kinds and their family recipes. I've never been allowed to pay for any of it.

I've learned that any time spent with a waterman is an experience never to be forgotten. Some days he'll keep you in stitches with his tall tales and keen wit. Other days you may learn something from him about equipment depreciation or the migratory habits of the blue crab. One thing's for sure . . . you'll never be bored. Like anyone else, there are good and bad among the watermen, but from what I've experienced, they represent one of God's best efforts. It's that good 99% that this book is about.

It helps to understand the Bay Waterman if you've known the fierce independence of a small Texas rancher or the honesty and love of country of the midwestern farmer. He wants only to work and be left alone. He's a good American and makes decisions with a quick, basic, no-nonsense logic. Given the authority, he could solve our country's problems in a few days, and for the life of him, doesn't understand why Washington can't.

He likes his fellow watermen. They're competitive, but ready to lend a hand when needed. He likes his boat, his dog, his truck and high seafood prices. He loves his mother, the water, his independence, his wife and children, and if he has grandchildren, you'll never see a bigger fool about anything, since he got his first boat. He dislikes nettles, meddling government people, the price of fuel and anyone who'd steal a pot.

There's no in between about his engine. He either loves it, "Ain't a finer motor ever been set into a boat than this one. We've run many a mile, me and her, singing to one another . . ." or he hates it, "I'm going to have this no account piece of junk melted down and beat out into a coffin, 'cause when they lay me out, it'll be this bastard that put me there".

He tolerates summer people, even though they get in his way a bit. He knows that they're good for his market and for the economy of his community. "I wouldn't mind them summer people so much if they'd bring more of them pretty girls down here and leave some of them fat old sooks to home". He has an eye for the ladies and is a constant flirt in their presence. It's not unusual for him to veer several hundred yards off course to get a better look at one.

He enjoys little children, especially around the docks. He grew up playing there himself. He's tolerant of their pranks and childish ways, but he's quick to reprimand them for dangerous foolishness, "My God in heaven, ain't you got no sense boy? . . . when them gears get holt of you, they ain't got no pity." He doesn't hesitate to show his affection for his own children, and its not unusual to see them touching and holding one another. He says he wants a better life for them than the water can give. Yet, as sincere as he might be, there's no prouder father than the one whose son tonged more oysters than anyone else at day's end.

He's a storyteller without equal and possesses a beautiful sense of humor. His descriptions are elaborate and colorful and not always printable. Even a simple "yes" comes out "Oh yes, my Lord" or "Well, now I guarantee you, cap'n".

He's strong and sensitive. He's aware of the beauty around him and of the things that endanger it. He talks about it often and his speech is sprinkled with words like "love" and "beautiful". He'll tell you of crying, because to him its not an indication of weakness, but of the severity of the situation.

He knows God, calls on him when in need and gives thanks.

We had finished, the old waterman and I . . . his catch loaded into refrigerated trucks and on it's way to market in some distant city. We tied up along side the other work boats and sat on the washboard chatting in the warm yellow light of late afternoon. "So you're going to put all of this down in a book with pictures of what goes on out here, are you?" . . . "Yes sir" . . . "And you think somebody might want to look at it and read what we say, do you?" "Yes sir, I hope so" . . . "Well, if things don't work out for you, you come on back and I'll put you to work. With a little practice, you might turn out to be a right fair culling boy". He chuckled and winked again.

I thanked him for his kindness and for letting me spend the day aboard. I didn't think much about his offer at the time, but as this project comes to a close, I can't think of anything I'd rather do.

"Morning's the prettiest time of day around here. We probably see more sunrises in a month than most people see in a lifetime."

"I like going out. You never know what's going to be in your nets. Sometimes it ain't much, but I enjoy going anyway."

"You know, people who work jobs in the city are always having to go someplace to unwind. Around here, we go to work to unwind. There's nothing more peaceful than getting out on the water by yourself."

"I enjoy going out by myself. Heading out on a pretty morning by yourself makes you feel close to your Maker and glad to be alive."

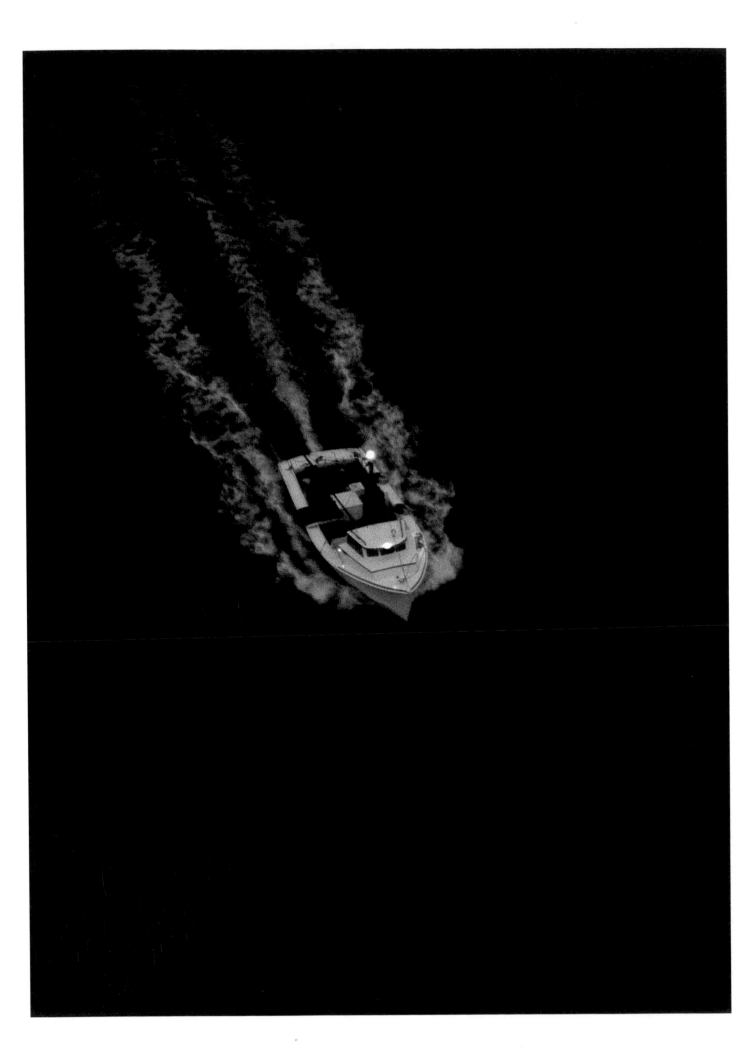

"It all depends on what you're doing and how the tide is running. Some mornings you're finished and home by ten o'clock . . . other days you won't get in 'till dark."

"When the haul seine boats really have a catch, they'll send someone ashore to call the ice truck. He'll load up and go across the island blowing his horn so everybody'll know to get up and go help with getting the fish in."

"Used to be, you couldn't fish for the blowfish. Now I never see one. No sooner people learned to eat 'em than they disappeared. That used to be a funny sight, this boat loaded up with them blowed up toads."

"Some fellow from the mountains come down here one time years back, and don't you know he thought we just went out with a dip net and dipped up whatever kind of fish we was after that day. He was a fellow that picked apples up there for a living you see and he didn't know nothing about the water. I told him, 'You have to work at it a little harder than that' ".

"I lose a lot that drop out when I'm getting in the nets. It don't bother me so much when they're alive, but when they're dead, they ain't doing nobody no good."

"You'll always get a good run of fish on the full moon."

"She was so loaded that a mouse could have set on the board and drank water."

"Some places they suck the fish out with a pipe. Down here we still use a shovel."

"I bet I've shoveled enough fish to fill the Queen Mary several times over."

"Just the two hundred poles for my nets cost $1,300. They might last me two seasons if the ice doesn't take 'em out."

"Those yachts run through my nets several times a season and cut 'em all to pieces. I've never had one of them come forward and tell me he'd done it and wanted to pay for the damages. I had one call me one time and tell me he'd gotten his wheel all tangled up in my nets and was pretty sure it had done some damage to his shaft or something, and what was I going to do about it. I told him what he could do with his shaft, wheel and all."

"I'm eighty five years old now and I go out with my boys nearly every day. I ain't as much help as I used to be, and people are always after me to leave it alone, but I'll tell you what . . . The human body is just like any machine . . . if you let it just set around and don't use it, it's going to get stiff and useless."

"These older men who've retired from the water still come down here every day to help us and see how we're doing. If we have a good day they're as happy as if they had caught 'em themselves. But it don't matter how good we do, one of 'em can almost always tell us how we could have done better."

"The only thing I don't like about the water is that I'm too old to work it any more."

"When a man's worked the water all his life, he'll keep coming back, even if its just to sit around the dock."

"Whatever you do on the water, its going to be the hard
   way to go.

"I envy the energy of these young boys. They can work
   along side me all day and when I'm too tired to get out of
   a chair, they're cleaned up and heading out."

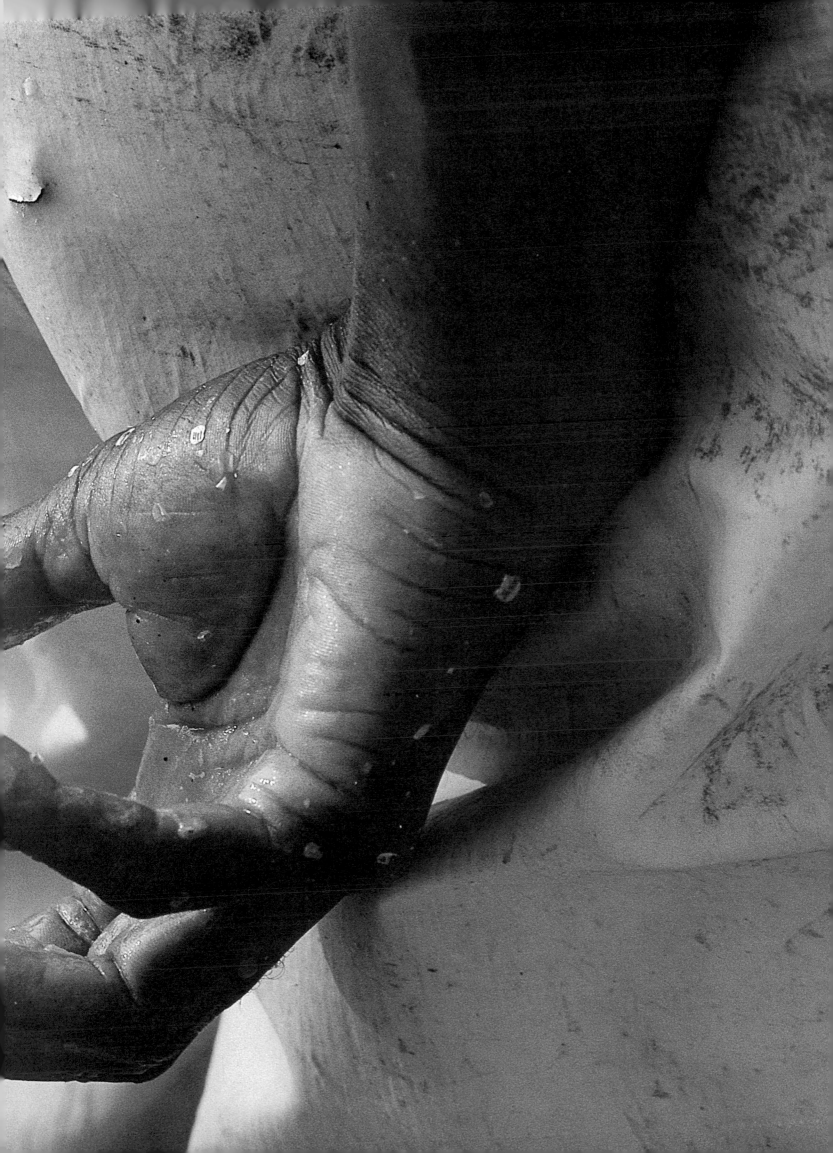

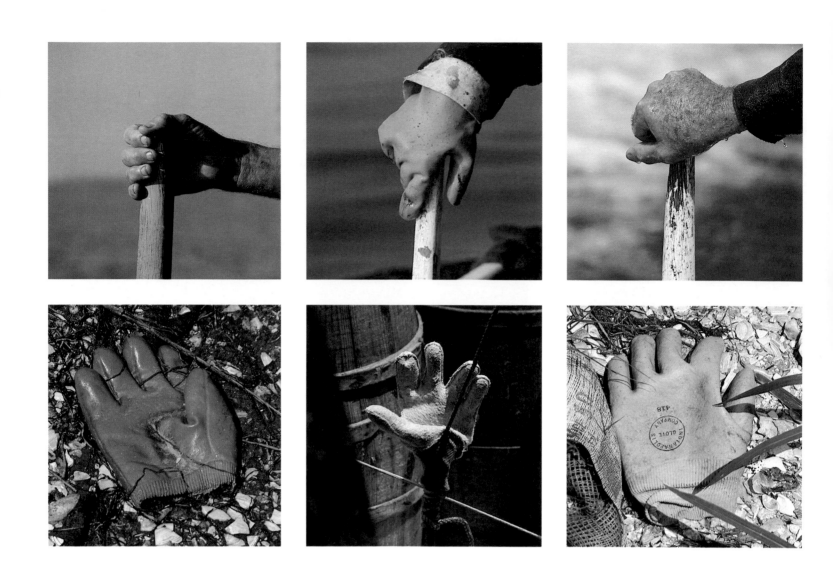

"It takes a lot of money to keep a boat like this up. There's always something breaking down and Lord, the cost of everything has gone out of sight. Now when you work on wages, all you got to take care of is your hands."

"I can't keep a pair of gloves a week."

"A man's hands catch hell out here in the summer from nettles, fish fins and crab pinchers. In the winter they just crack open by themselves."

"I split 'em and salt 'em overnight. Then I boil 'em for breakfast. You take a little bacon drippings and pepper and put on 'em and you'll never eat better fish."

"Well, they ain't bringing 'em back and they ain't complaining much and they keep on ordering more, so I guess I'm still making 'em O.K."

"I build them mostly by eye and feel these days. Don't do nearly as much measuring as I used to."

"Some name their boats for their wife, but most are named
for a daughter, I believe."

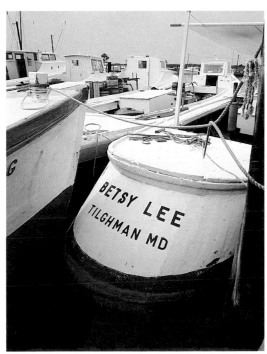

"You could run her a long time 'fore she'd leave you."

"She ain't never been right in the stern. I would take her back to the man what built her, but he died and I can't get him to do a thing."

"A real bad feeling come over me when I stepped off her for
the last time. You own a boat long enough and she gets to
be a part of you."

"She leakes a little. Woman on a fishing party told me, said
'it scares me when I hear that pump come on.' I told her,
'lady, it scares me when I don't hear it come on.' "

"When I sold her, it like to killed me. Some folks buy and
sell boats like they do automobiles, but when I've had
a boat for a while, I get awfully attached to her."

"I had a good business going painting houses . . . had several boys working for me and all, and a long list of people waiting for me to do their houses, but it got on my nerves so bad I had to give it up and go back to the water."

"I've worked jobs in the city several times, but I always come back . . . there's just something in me won't let me leave it alone."

"I didn't pay a whole lot of attention to things around here
till I came out of the hospital. I was so happy to be back
and able to work that everything out here looked extra
beautiful. I stop and watch the sun come up every morning
now."

"She was so rotten you could eat her with a spoon."

"My father had a log canoe that he used out here for twenty-six years. He was one of the last watermen around here that still used a canoe with a one lung Palmer in it. Mama said she always liked that engine 'cause she could walk out on the porch and tell about where he was. What's left of that boat is still up there in the creek. It always makes me a little sad whenever I see it."

"One thing that you'll never lack for when you're doing motor work and that's advice."

"You need arms like Oliveoil to get in here around this motor."

"I'm going to have this no account piece of junk melted down and beat out into a coffin, cause when they lay me out, it'll be this bastard that put me there."

"These conch and welk are some of the finest eating comes
out of the bay. You grind 'em up and stew 'em with some
onion and potato and a little salt and pepper and you got
something good."

"I ain't never ate no conch, not that I know of anyhow.
They tell me most of it ends up in clam chowder."

"The crab's a loner by nature, but that's just his way."

"I put out $3,000 worth of pots this spring. I'll be lucky if I still got half of them by August."

"I've worked a lot of jobs around, some of them paid pretty
   good, but every summer, as soon as I heard that somebody
   had caught a hundred dollars worth of crabs, I'd quit and
   go to crabbing."

"Most of these whities go to Philadelphia and most of the sooks to New York. Baltimore won't take much other than the number one jimmies. They know their crabs, those Baltimore people do."

"The farmer's a lucky man, not to have to put up with nettles. 'Course we ain't too bothered by Johnson grass."

"I don't mind a few on my arms, but I got to keep 'em away from my eyes. You get a piece in your eye, you'll think a pistol bullet struck you."

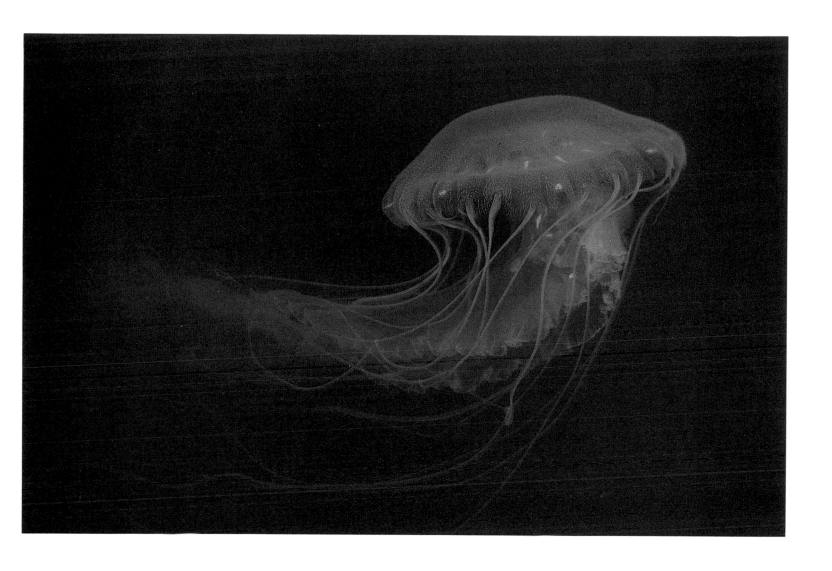

"Oh yes my, Lord . . . it'd be easy to get rid of those nettles
. . . just find somebody that'd pay five cents a pound for
'em and they'd disappear as fast as the blow toads did."

"Man from the institute down there asked me the other day
if I was catching more of anything than I used to . . . I told
him yea . . . sea nettles."

"When the water's this calm and clear, they won't stay on
the bait long enough for you to net them. They'll fly off
every which way like a bunch of nervous jack rabbits."

"Sometimes you might get two bushels on one lick and two
crabs on the next one. There ain't no way of telling. It's
about worked out around here though."

"We've dredged up some strange things. Everything from a dead man to a woman's pocketbook with ninety-seven dollars in it."

"To hell with some pots. My God, you're never
finished when you're potting, with all the moving 'em and
cleaning 'em, putting 'em in and taking 'em out."

"Lord, look at the crabs. We laid into a whole herd of 'em today."

"Those sooks get wild toward the fall of the year. They'll tear up a pot or a net or anything gets around 'em, including another crab. Only thing I know meaner in the bay is a bluefish."

"Every time the crabbers have a bad year, they start blaming it on people taking sponge crabs. They write to their representatives and to the Resources Commission and raise all sorts of hell. The next year crabbing picks up and they forget all about the sponge crab."

"I don't guess it makes a lot of difference . . . they been dredging crabs out of the bottom and cooking sponge crabs down there for a hundred years and I swear, I think we got more crabs now than I ever seen."

"I've never seen as many pots as there are out there this year. A crab would have to sidestep every few feet to make it up the river. Somebody set one right on top of one of mine the other day."

"Some days I think the crabs the dumbest creature on earth . . . other days I know he's outsmarting me."

"This red water will kill a crab. If they're in the pot when the red water comes in, you'll pull up a pot full of dead ones."

"I never saw anybody put his pots so close together. He could fish two of 'em off his boat at the same time. I told him, you don't set your pots, you sew 'em."

"You can go ahead of a man who's good at this and if you don't cloud up the water, he'll catch more than you do."

"When you find pots where they're not supposed to be, they've usually been set out by summer people. It's easy to tell when you pull 'em up . . . no zink, no weight and chicken backs for bait."

"I've been watching 'em shed all my life, but it still amazes
me every time I see it."

"They're pretty now, but they ain't so pretty in the middle
of the night when you got to get up and come down here."

"I was working with a man some years back and there was a good run on peeler crabs. We shed out four hundred dozen crabs in twenty-four hours, just him and his wife and myself."

"People know I make good money shedding crabs, but what a lot of them don't know is that you got to work at it. These fellows that check their floats in the afternoon and then leave them 'till morning aren't going to be in business long. They may sell some of those papershells for soft once but that's about it."

"Some people break the pincher, but there ain't no need to do that. Just look for that pink line on his backfin to turn red . . . then you'll know he's getting ready to bust."

"People call me a heavy baiter, but when I hit on some crabs, I want to stay there and catch 'em . . . the big ones ain't going to dine with you if you skimp on the food."

"Most people sell you some eel, they'll weight up what you want and then throw in a handfull. That old guy's so tight that if that scale is a half ounce over, he'll cut the tail off one."

"Those foreigners are getting all the good eel. All they're leaving for us around here any more is shoe strings."

"If it don't pick up, you going to see some long faces around
    here."

"This takes one strong back, one weak mind and two fast hands."

"Now right here where we is, the oysters are as clean and pure as can be, but no sooner you cross the line from that marker there to shore, and them oysters over there ain't fit for human consumption. Now you explain that to me, will you, when the same tide passes over both of them every day."

"I think the government people are worrying about this pollution business too much. The Lord gave everything an apparatus for purifying what it eats. We used to use horse meat for crab bait, but the crab didn't taste like horse."

"These clams come up from a polluted section of the James.
We dump them overboard here between these flags and in
about a month tong them back up, good as new."

"Those boys from down in Gloucester they call guineamen are some of the best watermen on this bay. My father and I tonged right beside one this last fall and if we tonged thirty bushels between us, he'd tong fifty by himself."

"I was 11 when my mother died and my father got sick
hauling fish up the bay and had to go into the hospital in
Baltimore. There was four of us children at home and I was
the oldest. I was in the fourth grade and I quit and went to
work cause somebody had too. I've worked ever since then
and I'll be sixty-eight this fall. There's been some hard
times but I've loved every minute of it. My only regret is
that I wasn't around to spend more time with my children.
I quit dredging last year and it was the first winter I've
spent at home in forty years."

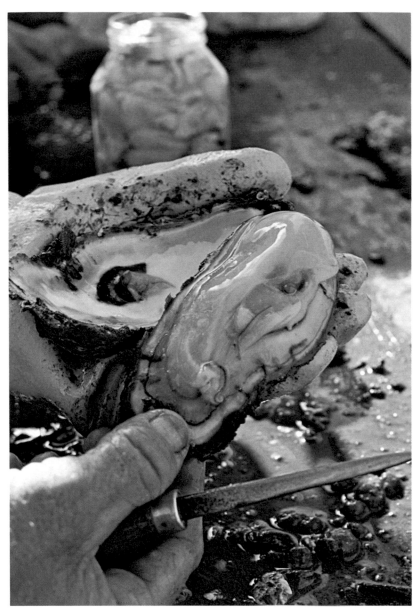

"A fellow shucking oysters for a man in Crisfield found the prettiest pearl you ever saw in one. He handed it over to the boss and the man turned around and fired him. Said he didn't want nobody that stupid working for him."

"I've heard it said, it was a brave man that ate the first raw oyster."

"I like to oyster better than crabbing. Oysters ain't always running off where you got to go find 'em again."

"When its a foggy night and someone hasn't come in,
they'll start blowing the siren at the fire house so he'll
know which way is home."

"She laid froze up right there for over two months and I didn't tong oyster one. People always trying to say the watermen makes a lot of money cause he can catch a couple hundred dollars worth of something in a day, but they ain't thinking about all those days that I can't go out cause of the weather or when I do go out and don't catch enough to pay for my gas. They ain't thinking about what it cost to put out 200 crab pots or set a pound net or have a boat built or overhaul a diesel . . . not to mention the time you loose doing it. If we're doing so well, where are all the big cars and big houses. Hell, some years, I'd be better off on welfare."

"When I was sixteen, I got my first pair of tongs and went to oystering. They were bringing forty cents a bushel and that first day, I brought in three bushels. I went all over town with my girl that night and couldn't spend that money. We went to the movies, had popcorn and a drink and then went for ice cream. I still went home with thirty cents in my pocket."

"You know, there might be twelve boats oystering out of this creek now . . . I can remember when there was two hundred and as many as fifteen buy boats at the mouth of the creek. They were so thick, you could walk from one to the other and sometimes they had to open a chanel for the oystering boats to come in."

"When I was 14, my daddy was doing carpentry work 10 hours a day for 40¢ an hour and my mother was working in town for seven dollars a week. I never did care for school much, so I quit and bought an old boat for ten dollars. For another ten, I got a motor to go in her and I went to oystering. It sort of come natural to me and I was doing OK with oysters bringing twenty five cents a bushel. Then they started going up and one day when I come in, they were paying a dollar a bushel. I had seventeen bushels and when I got home and showed them the money, my daddy said to hell with carpentry and he went to oystering too."

"He can make just about anything the waterman needs,
that fellow can. Somebody'll get a new piece of equipment
and he'll go study it, cause if it works, a lot of people'll
be wanting one too. Chances are, the one he builds will
be better than the one you can buy in Baltimore."

"My father bought this store in 1928. The watermen from
 Bull Island used to spend the weeknights down here on
 their boats. Everybody didn't have cars back in those days,
 so they only got home on weekends. This was their social
 gathering place and my father would stay down here some
 nights till ten o'clock while they talked and gossiped and
 told stories. They could keep you spellbound with their
 stories."

"I've been coming to this store for 50 years and the only
 thing that's changed is the prices."

"You'll never eat better food than what you eat on board a boat, for some reason I don't know, everything taste better on the water."

"I never seen anything eat like them boys. If you didn't stop them, they'd eat the cabin right off her."

"My wife would get up and cook for me any morning, but
somedays I'd rather come down here and eat with the
boys. Its that way with most everybody."

"Now that one there, he's a pretty good cook but I'd sure
hate to have to live with that ugly face 'round my house."

"My wife's the best cook I know. She can even cook better than my mother. My daughter-in-law can cook a lot of that fancy stuff but don't none of it taste as good as my wife's cooking."

"Some nights I can't sleep in the house. I get my clothes on and come down here and sleep on board. My wife don't understand it, but I swear, I'd rather sleep on board this boat than in the Chamberlayne Hotel."

"These boys will talk about one another and fight among themselves, but you let an outsider come in here and start something and you never saw a bunch stick closer together in your life."

"One of the fellows that drinks right heavy lost his teeth overboard one day. The boys were funning with him and one told him to drop a half pint over on a string and he'd bring 'em up."

"You could never out do that fellow. I told him one day after a bad squall come through here, I said "where we was, it blew so hard, it started a sea in our water jug" and he said 'I speck that's the truth, cause I left one of them little 3-in-1 oil cans on the motor box and it rained so hard, it filled her up' ".

"Men are always talking about women gossiping . . . My Lord, a woman can't hold a candle to a man when it comes to gossip. They get down on those boats of theirs and talk about everything and everybody."

"Those tax boys will have you scratching your head when it don't itch."

"When that man came to see me it liked to scared me to death. I asked him into the dining room and we both took a chair. My Lord, he was as cool as a cucumber. He took off his plaid sport coat, laid it over a chair, rolled up his sleeves, laid all his papers out in neat little piles, and cleared his throat. I was sitting over there with a death grip on my chair arms and sweat rolling off of me big as green peas. Don't you know, he'd been back to the foundation. He knew everything about my bank account and everything. He says to me "As I see it, you owe us $1,800", I said "Hell, man, I ain't worth that much, but we'll square it up". Come to find out, some of the tax he charged me was on money I'd already paid tax on. I'd been saving money around the house for about forty years 'til my wife made me put it in the bank. Then I had no way to prove where that money come from or that I'd paid tax on it."

"They say it's bad luck to let anyone come on board with a black suitcase or a black walnut. Some of the old captains wouldn't ever let a woman come out on a workboat... figured it was bad luck. I'm not too superstitious myself but I hate to see a hatch cover or a culling board turned bottom upwards... a shovel's the same way. If it happens on a boat I'm on, I'll reach and turn it right... I just always heard it was a bad sign."

"I've heard tell that it's bad luck if a crow flies over your boat. It's O.K. if it's two of them though."

"It's bad luck to bring a chicken aboard a boat."

"You won't see much blue on boats on this island. Most people around here think its bad luck. A fellow I know let them paint a blue boot stripe on his boat when he hauled her. The first day of oyster season, every thing that could go wrong did. It scared him so bad that he had her hauled again just to paint over that boot stripe. I know another fellow I was working with one day couldn't keep his engine running right. It was coughing and spitting and skipping and when he raised up the cover he saw that the engine had a blue oil cap. He threw it overboard and she never missed again the rest of the day. I don't put a lot of stock in that mess, but then I don't paint no blue on my boat either."

"When I was getting ready to get married, I went to Easton to get her a wedding dress and came home with a blue one. She wouldn't get married in it... made me go back and trade it for a white one. We had to put the wedding off a week."

"People on the water watch out for one another. If one man's got something that another one needs, he don't have to bargain with him over it . . . I might need a few of a man's peelers to go fishing and the next week he might want a few of my clams to take home."

"There's one thing about the people on this island, white or colored, you'll never see nobody want for nothing. Everybody looks after one another."

"When a man's in trouble, anybody here abouts will risk his life for him, don't matter what he thinks of him."

"I worked awhile in Richmond and some other places where people hardly knew one another . . . and didn't much care. Here on the water, now we all know each other and we all care about one another. Guess that's why I decided to stay a waterman."

"Sometimes it looks like most of the men around here are older men and I wonder if there'll be enough young ones to carry on when we're gone . . . so many of them going to work in town and all. It always makes me feel good to see a young man's face on one of these boats."

"No, my boy says he ain't going to mess with the water . . .
don't see no reason to punish hisself that way."

"I used to love to go out with my father in the summer.
We'd sit up on the motor box and talk about all sorts of
things. He's 71 and still working and I'm still learning
things from him."

"My granddaddy used to bring me down here as a boy. He taught me near about everything I know about the water."

"In the summer these docks are like a playground for the waterman's kids . . . I enjoy having them around."

"My father used to say when young boys were working together. "One boy's worth about one boy and two boys are worth about a half a boy. Three boy's ain't worth having around.""

"I guess city people wonder what we do down here for entertainment, since there's not a disco or a movie house every half mile. During the week there's not a whole lot going on, but on the weekend there's almost always a dance around somewhere or somebody's having a party. If nothing else is going on, sometimes we'll get our dates to pack up a picnic and we'll head over to Silver Beach."

"I never saw much sense in going to college. Once you get the education, you got to go to the city to get a good job and once you've lived here, you'll never want to live in the city."

"I'll tell you how to raise a child. You teach him a love for God and his Church. You show him fairness and honesty and he can't help but grow up right."

"Sure, I thought I would have liked for my daughter to marry a doctor or lawyer, but there's only one doctor in this county and he's married and sixty years old. When she was seventeen she told me she wanted to marry this boy who was a waterman. I tried to talk her into waiting but it won't no use. Now I tell you, he's a hard working boy . . . he's good to his family and he don't drink. I got me two of the prettiest grandchildren you ever saw and when they come up to the house, me and him's got something to talk about. Hell, I wouldn't know what to say to a lawyer."

"I've always enjoyed giving. Whatever I got, its the greatest
pleasure I know to share it with other people that need it
or don't have any. You know, when it's all said and done,
the only thing you got is what you gave away...You
can't take nothing else with you."

"And we pray that you will help us through these troubled times, for we know that in all things you do, there is a purpose."

"Eternal Father, strong to save, Whose arm hath bound the restless wave, Who bidst the mighty ocean deep, Its own appointed limits keep: O hear us when we cry to thee, For those in peril on the sea."

"Amen"